The Magic School Bus
in the Time
of the Dinosaurs

The Magic School Bus
in the Time of the Dinosaurs

By Joanna Cole
Illustrated by Bruce Degen

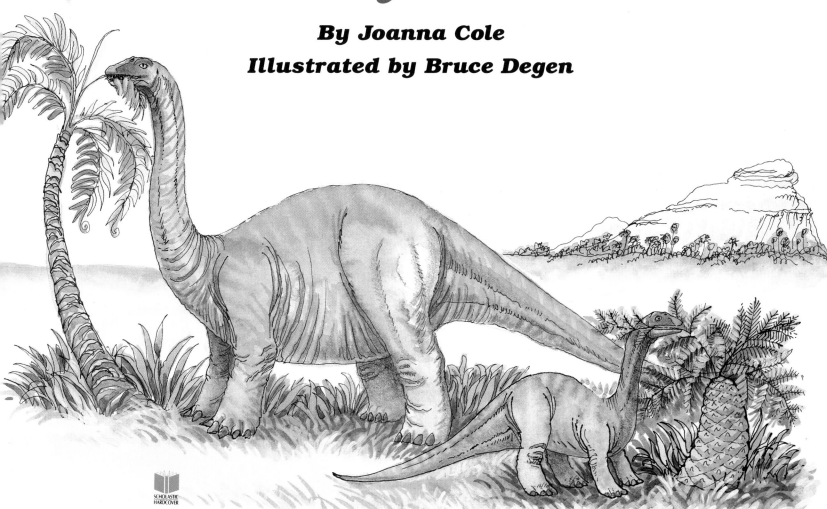

SCHOLASTIC
HARDCOVER

SCHOLASTIC INC. / *New York*

*The author and illustrator wish to thank
Mark A. Norell, Associate Curator of Vertebrate Paleontology,
the American Museum of Natural History, for his assistance in preparing this book.*

*For their helpful advice and consultation, thanks also to Armand Morgan,
Public Education Department, Yale-Peabody Museum of Natural History, New Haven, Connecticut;
Professor Leo J. Hickey, Curator of Paleobotany, Yale-Peabody Museum of Natural History;
Dave Varricchio, expert of Tyrannosaurus Rex, Museum of the Rockies, Bozeman, Montana.*

Library of Congress Cataloging-in-Publication Data

Cole, Joanna.
The magic school bus: in the time of the dinosaurs / written by
Joanna Cole; illustrated by Bruce Degen.
p.   cm.
ISBN 0-590-44688-6
1. Dinosaurs — Pictorial works — Juvenile literature.
[1. Dinosaurs.] I. Degen, Bruce, ill. II. Title.
QE862.D5C694   1994
567.9'1 — dc20   93-5753
CIP
AC

12 11 10 9 8   5 6 7 8 9/9

Printed in the U.S.A.   37

First printing, September 1994

The illustrator used pen and ink, watercolor, color pencil,
and gouache for the paintings in this book.

To Armand Morgan,
our personal guide to the time of the dinosaurs
J.C. & B.D.

It was Visitors Day at our school.
Parents, relatives, and friends
were coming that afternoon to see our work.
In Ms. Frizzle's class, we were making
the whole room into Dinosaur Land!

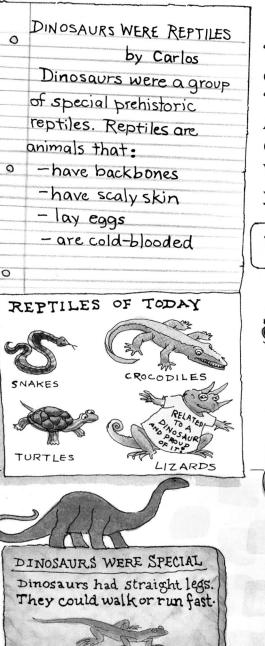

DINOSAURS WERE REPTILES
by Carlos

Dinosaurs were a group of special prehistoric reptiles. Reptiles are animals that:
- have backbones
- have scaly skin
- lay eggs
- are cold-blooded

REPTILES OF TODAY

SNAKES

CROCODILES

TURTLES

RELATED TO A DINOSAUR AND PROUD OF IT!

LIZARDS

DINOSAURS WERE SPECIAL
Dinosaurs had straight legs. They could walk or run fast.

Today's reptiles have sprawled-out legs.

"Our class has been invited to a dinosaur dig," explained the Friz.
"We'll be leaving right away."
As we went out, one kid grabbed the video camera.
Others took along model dinosaurs for good luck.
When you have the wackiest teacher in school,
you need all the luck you can get!

WE'RE LEAVING NOW?

I GUESS MS. FRIZZLE FORGOT ABOUT VISITORS DAY.

SHE NEVER FORGOT ANYTHING BEFORE.

Dear dig, Come and see the dinosaur bones we're digging up. Bring the whole class. Yours, Jeff

Ms. V. Frizzle SCHOOL U.S.A.

We couldn't believe we had to get on that rickety old school bus again. Kids held their lucky dinosaurs tight, and hoped for the best.

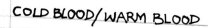

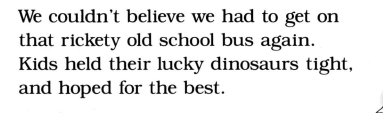

NO PEOPLE EVER SAW
A DINOSAUR   by Florrie
When early humans
appeared on earth,
dinosaurs had already
been dead for millions
of years!
People found out about
dinosaurs from fossils.

FIVE KINDS OF DINOSAUR
FOSSILS   by Alex

1. BONES

2. TEETH

3. FOOTPRINTS

4. SKIN PRINTS

5. EGGS AND
   NESTS

As we rolled onto the highway,
Ms. Frizzle shouted from the driver's seat,
"We're on our way to fossil country, kids!
Who knows what a fossil is?"
Luckily, we had done our homework.
We knew a fossil is anything left
from a prehistoric animal or plant.

THIS STORY
IS
MAKE-BELIEVE.

THERE WERE NO
DINOSAURS IN
THE TIME OF
CAVE PEOPLE.

After we had been driving for a long time,
we came to a desert where people were working.
Ms. Frizzle said this was the dinosaur dig.
The people were paleontologists —
scientists who study prehistoric life.

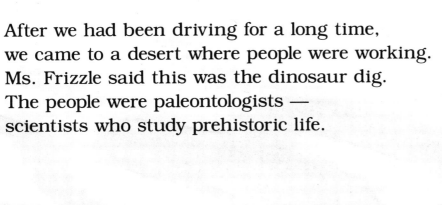

DINOSAURS LASTED FOR 150 MILLION YEARS ON EARTH! WEREN'T THEY AMAZING, ARNOLD?

IT'S AMAZING THAT I'VE LASTED THIS LONG IN MS. FRIZZLE'S CLASS.

HOW A DEAD DINOSAUR COULD BECOME A FOSSIL
by Carmen

1. The dead body sank in a river, and rotted away.

2. The bones were covered with sand.

3. In time, the sand turned into rocks.

4. The bones became hard as rock, too.

DID MOST DINOSAURS TURN INTO FOSSILS?

NO! DEAD DINOSAURS USUALLY ROTTED OR WERE EATEN.

DINOSAURS WERE SPECIAL
Dinosaurs were on earth 1500 times longer than humans have been so far.

We saw a gleam in Ms. Frizzle's eye.
"Want to look for some *Maiasaura* nests,
kids?" she shouted.
She rushed us onto the bus
and drove off.

We hadn't gone far when Ms. Frizzle
stopped the bus.
She turned a dial on the dashboard,
and the bus began to change.
It looked like a giant alarm clock.
Ms. Frizzle said it was a time machine!

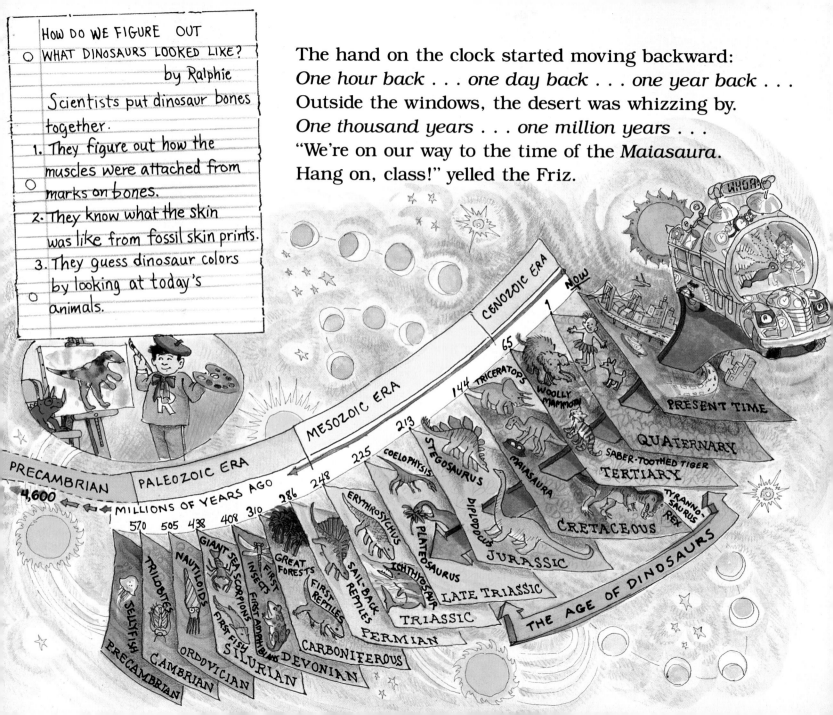

The hand on the clock started moving backward:
One hour back . . . one day back . . . one year back . . .
Outside the windows, the desert was whizzing by.
One thousand years . . . one million years . . .
"We're on our way to the time of the *Maiasaura*.
Hang on, class!" yelled the Friz.

FOSSIL TEETH TELL WHAT DINOSAURS ATE
by Phoebe

Sharp, pointy teeth came from meat-eaters.

TROODON
ALLOSAURUS
TYRANNOSAURUS REX

BRUSHING KEEPS YOUR TEETH IN SHAPE
WHATEVER SHAPE THEY ARE

Odd-shaped teeth came from plant-eaters.

STEGOSAURUS
PLATEOSAURUS
CAMARASAURUS

The Friz pointed to some dinosaurs that were hunting on the banks of a river. "Their name is *Coelophysis*," she said. "These early dinosaurs were small and light. The giant dinosaurs did not develop until later."

COELOPHYSIS HAVE EXCELLENT TEETH FOR EATING MEAT. THEIR TEETH HAVE "SAW" EDGES LIKE STEAK KNIVES.

TRY NOT TO LOOK LIKE A STEAK!

PREY:
DRAGONFLY
LIZARD
MAMMALS
AMPHIBIAN

Suddenly, a large reptile rose out of the water and opened its huge mouth.
"That is not a dinosaur," Ms. Frizzle said.
"It's a phytosaur — a crocodile-like reptile."
The phytosaur caught a little dinosaur and pulled it underwater.
We wanted to get back on the bus, pronto!
But Ms. Frizzle said we had to learn about Triassic plant life.

AETOSAUR

PHYTOSAUR

ARE MEAT-EATERS MEAN?
by Arnold
No. Predators are part of nature. Hunting is the only way they can get their food.

SOME WORDS FROM DOROTHY ANN
A predator is a hunting animal.
Prey are the animals a predator hunts.

I'M A PREDATOR.

I'M PREY.

TRIASSIC PLANTS
by John

In Triassic times
you would see:

Horsetails   Cycads   Ferns

Gingkos   Conifers

DINOSAURS WERE SPECIAL
Many dinosaurs were plant-eaters. Only a few kinds of modern reptiles are.

Plateosaur Tooth

GINGKOS

We were examining some ferns
when Ms. Frizzle shouted,
"Look at those terrific prosauropods!
They were the first dinosaurs to eat plants!"

I JUST LOVE TRIASSIC PLANTS, CLASS--DON'T YOU?

DO YOU HEAR SOMETHING?

YOU MEAN THOSE CRUNCHING SOUNDS?

MS. FRIZZLE ISN'T THE ONLY ONE WHO LOVES TRIASSIC PLANTS.

CYCADS

FERNS

ANCHISAURUS

CONIFER

PLATEOSAUR

A sudden downpour caught us by surprise.
But the dinosaurs went right on eating.
We ran for the bus, and Frizzie called,
"Get ready to go *forward* in time, kids!"

IN A TROPICAL FOREST, RAINS ARE FREQUENT AND HEAVY, ARNOLD.

NOW SHE TELLS ME!

JEFF WILL LOVE THIS VIDEO.

THE FIRST MAMMALS
LIVED WITH DINOSAURS
by Rachel

The first true mammals lived in the Late Triassic. They were furry rat-like animals.

WHAT ARE MAMMALS?
by Wanda

Mammals are animals that:
- have backbones
- have hair or fur
- are warm-blooded

- feed their babies with mothers' milk

The last things we saw before we took off
were some small, furry animals.
Ms. Frizzle said they were the first mammals.
The hand on the clock moved ahead,
and the Triassic rain forest whizzed out of sight.

WHEN WILL WE SEE MAIASAURA EGGS?

MAIASAURA LIVED 160 MILLION YEARS FROM NOW. LET'S SEE IF WE CAN FIND THEM.

NOW

THEN

LATER

EARLY MAMMALS

Ring! Ring! The alarm went off,
and we heard Ms. Frizzle say, "Oh no!"
We had stopped too soon.
It was the Late Jurassic Period,
the Age of Giants!

APATOSAURUS
(ALSO CALLED
BRONTOSAURUS)

HERE ARE SOME
INTERESTING
TREE TRUNKS.

UM... I DON'T
THINK SO.

WHAT WAS THE EARTH LIKE THEN?

Continents were drifting apart.
• Swampy, low-lying plains
○ Beginnings of inland seas
• Beginning of Atlantic Ocean
• Warm temperatures everywhere

WHERE WE ARE IN TIME

PRESENT TIME

CENOZOIC ERA
65 MILLION YEARS AGO

CRETACEOUS
144 MILLION YEARS AGO

JURASSIC
213 MILLION YEARS AGO

LATE TRIASSIC
225 MILLION YEARS AGO

WE KNOW DINOSAURS
O LAID EGGS
by Amanda Jane
Fossil dinosaur eggs have been found. Inside some, there are tiny skeletons of babies.

HOW BIG WERE DINOSAUR EGGS?
by Molly
The largest dinosaur egg we have found was about the size of a football!

Under a pile of leaves, we found some dinosaur eggs just about to hatch!
Nearby some stegosaurs — plated dinosaurs — were eating plants.
One of the stegosaurs had a hurt leg.

ARE THEY THE MAIASAURA EGGS?

NO, KEESHA. MAIASAURA DID NOT LIVE IN THE JURASSIC PERIOD.

THEY CAME LATER. MUCH LATER.

Suddenly an *Allosaurus* approached
the wounded *Stegosaurus*.
Stegosaurus's spiked tail lashed out.
It missed *Allosaurus* by an inch!
What would happen next?
We held our breath.

serrated edge

ALLOSAURUS
TOOTH
(actual size)

IT'S HARD TO BE A HUNTER
by Alex
Being a predator is
dangerous. Predators
can get hurt or killed
by their prey. This is why
meat-eaters often attack
prey that is weak, sick,
or young.

Allosaurus darted close and took a big bite.
Then it moved back and waited.
Stegosaurus got weaker and weaker.
It had become food for *Allosaurus*.

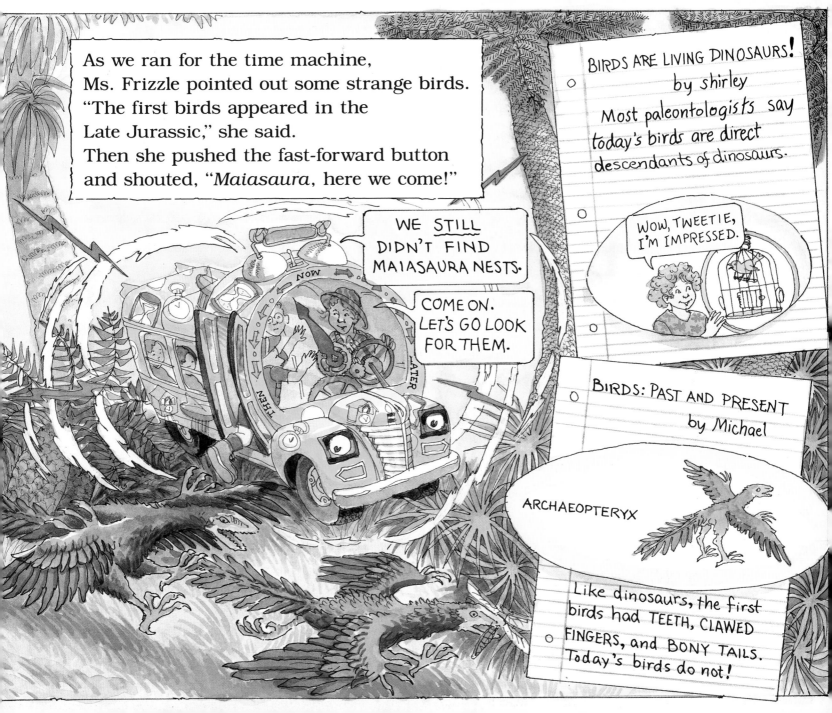

ALL DINOSAURS WERE LAND ANIMALS
by Gregory

No dinosaurs lived in the sea. During the Cretaceous, dinosaurs lived in places that were not covered by water.

WE WON'T SEE ANY DINOSAURS HERE.

Ring! Ring! The alarm went off again.
We looked out — and then we freaked out!
Once again, we had stopped too soon.
"Here we are in the Late Cretaceous Period,"
announced Ms. Frizzle.
"At this time there was a sea
right in the middle of our continent."

WE'RE IN THE SAME PLACE 25 MILLION YEARS LATER.

HOW TIME FLIES.

THAT'S NOT ALL THAT FLIES.

PTERANODON

WHERE WE ARE IN TIME

PRESENT TIME
CENOZOIC ERA 65 MILLION YEARS AGO
CRETACEOUS 144 MILLION YEARS AGO
JURASSIC 213 MILLION YEARS AGO
LATE TRIASSIC 225 MILLION YEARS AGO

Out the windows, enormous sea reptiles swam by.
Overhead, flying reptiles glided past,
dipping their beaks in the water to catch fish.
We were getting a little wet,
so the Friz set the clock ahead again.

As soon as we got off the bus,
we saw that the Cretaceous world was different.
The weather was cooler.
There were colorful flowers and fruits everywhere.
And there were lots of new plant-eating dinosaurs.
"These plant-eaters could chew better than
any other dinosaurs," said Ms. Frizzle.
"They had terrific teeth for grinding,
and they had *cheeks*!"

NEW PLANT-EATERS OF THE CRETACEOUS PERIOD
by Ms. Frizzle

DUCKBILLS
Had hundreds of teeth in horny beaks.

DOMEHEADS
Had thick skulls. May have butted heads like rams.

ARMORED
Had armor. Had few teeth.

HORNED
Had neck frill and horns. Had slicing teeth.

CHEEKS KEEP FOOD FROM FALLING OUT SO PLANT-EATERS DO NOT LOSE FOOD THEY HAVE ALREADY CHEWED.

GEE, I DIDN'T KNOW CHEEKS WERE SO IMPORTANT.

DINOSAURS WERE SPECIAL
Some dinosaurs chewed their food. All of today's reptiles swallow it whole.

DUCKBILL TEETH
Duckbills had hundreds of rows of teeth.

The tyrannosaurs were scary enough.
Then a pack of *Troodon* showed up, too!
They were small, but there were a lot of them!
They began circling the bus to see what it was.
We sized up the situation and ran.

I HOPE YOU ARE OBSERVING THE TROODON, CLASS. NOTICE THE SLASHING CLAW ON EACH BACK FOOT.

WE'D LIKE TO OBSERVE THEM, MS. FRIZZLE, BUT...

WE HAVE TO LEAVE... RIGHT AWAY.

IN A HURRY...

THIS INSTANT...

IN OTHER WORDS... NOW!

TROODON

ALL MEAT-EATING DINOSAURS WERE TWO-LEGGED
by Phoebe
Plant-eaters came in all different shapes.

Hadrosaurus Stegosaurus Apatosaurus
But all meat-eaters were built on the same pattern.

Allosaurus
Coelophysis Tyrannosaurus Rex

Troodon Tooth (actual size)

DINOSAURS WERE SPECIAL
Some dinosaurs may have hunted in packs!
None of today's reptiles do.

As we came over the crest of a hill,
we saw an incredible sight!
It was the *Maiasaura* nesting ground!

WHY DO WE THINK MAIASAURA BABIES GREW UP IN NESTS?

by Wanda

When scientists found the first Maiasaura nests, they saw:

- Crushed eggshells, showing that babies might have stayed in nests and stepped on shells.
- Skeletons of different sizes, showing that babies might have grown bigger in nests.

- Worn down baby teeth, showing that babies might have eaten food brought by parents.

We weren't the only ones
who had found the *Maiasaura*.
The *Troodon* had followed us.
They invaded the nesting ground.
The *Maiasaura* parents defended their young.
All at once, a sandstorm blew up.
In minutes, a thick layer of sand
covered the dinosaurs.

Everything happened so fast.
There was no way we could help
the dinosaurs.
Maybe they would become fossils.

OH, NO!
I DROPPED
MY MODEL
MAIASAURA!

HURRY UP
AND RUN!

Back in the bus, Ms. Frizzle drove
forward in time.
We thought we were going home,
but, on the way,
the bus screeched to a stop.

STRUTHIOMIMUS

PRESENT TIME

CENOZOIC ERA
65 MILLION YEARS AGO

CRETACEOUS
144 MILLION YEARS AGO

JURASSIC
213 MILLION YEARS AGO

LATE TRIASSIC
225 MILLION YEARS AGO

WHERE WE ARE IN TIME

"We are in the very last minutes of the Cretaceous Period," said Ms. Frizzle. A bright light was shining in the sky. "Notice that asteroid," said the Friz. "It's a huge rock from outer space. Soon it will hit the earth."

THE ASTEROID WILL CAUSE AN ENORMOUS EXPLOSION... BLACK SOOT WILL FILL THE AIR AND BLOCK OUT THE SUN... PLANTS WON'T GROW, AND MILLIONS OF LIVING THINGS WILL BECOME EXTINCT — INCLUDING THE DINOSAURS.

MS. FRIZZLE, COULD WE LEAVE BEFORE THE ASTEROID HITS?

LAMBEOSAURUS

The Friz pushed the forward button, and we started again.

WE'RE ONLY 65 MILLION YEARS FROM HOME, CLASS.

STEP ON IT, PLEASE...

When the alarm rang, we were back in our own time.
The paleontologists were worried about us,
and came looking for us.
We gave them a tip on a fossil site.
Then we waved good-bye and drove back to school.

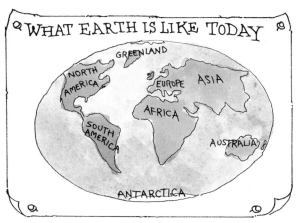

In the classroom, we made a chart
of our trip to the dinosaurs.
Just as we were finishing it,
people started coming in for Visitors Day.

The visitors admired everything.
They had never seen such fabulous projects,
such wonderful books, or such an incredible video.
And, of course, they had never met a teacher
quite like Ms. Frizzle!

YOUR BONES ARE THE BEST, HONEY.

THANKS, GRAN.

HEY, LOOK AT THOSE SPECIAL EFFECTS!

THE DINOSAURS SEEM SO REAL!

WHY FLORRIE, THIS READS AS IF YOU WERE REALLY THERE.

IT OUGHT TO.

VCR TAPE PLAYER

MODEL OF DINOSAUR SKELETON by Phoebe Made from Chicken bones and clay

THE DAY I MET A MAIASAURA by Florrie